T0099150

PAST AND FUTURE YELLOWSTONES

PAST AND FUTURE YELLOWSTONES

FINDING OUR WAY IN WONDERLAND

Paul Schullery

THE UNIVERSITY OF UTAH PRESS

Salt Lake City

Publication of this keepsake edition is made possible in part by
The Wallace Stegner Center for Land, Resources and the Environment
S. J. Quinney College of Law
AND BY
The Special Collections Department
J. Willard Marriot Library

The Publisher gratefully acknowledges their generous support of this project.

Copyright © 2015 by The University of Utah Press.
All rights reserved.

This lecture was originally delivered on March 26, 2014, at the Nineteenth
Annual Symposium of the Wallace Stegner Center for Land, Resources
and the Environment.

The Defiance House Man colophon is a registered trademark of the
University of Utah Press. It is based on a four-foot-tall Ancient Puebloan
pictograph (late PIII) near Glen Canyon, Utah.

19 18 17 16 15   2 3 4 5

Cover image: *Grand Canyon of the Yellowstone* by Thomas Moran, courtesy of the
National Park Service

Interior photographs by Paul Schullery

FOREWORD

The Wallace Stegner Lecture serves as a public forum for addressing the critical environmental issues that confront society. Conceived in 2009 on the centennial of Wallace Stegner's birth, the lecture honors the Pulitzer prize–winning author, educator, and conservationist by bringing a prominent scholar, public official, advocate, or spokesperson to the University of Utah with the aim of informing and promoting public dialogue over the relationship between humankind and the natural world. The lecture is delivered in connection with the Wallace Stegner Center's annual symposium and published by the University of Utah Press to ensure broad distribution. Just as Wallace Stegner envisioned a more just and sustainable world, the lecture acknowledges Stegner's enduring conservation legacy by giving voice to "the geography of hope" that he evoked so eloquently throughout his distinguished career.

Robert B. Keiter, Director
WALLACE STEGNER CENTER FOR LAND,
RESOURCES AND THE ENVIRONMENT

Past and Future Yellowstones

The defining characteristic of the national park system—troubling to some, challenging to all—is the individuality of each unit. These places have been added to the system, we are often told, because they are unique. And they are unique, we discover, not only for their cultural, ecological, or geophysical character, but also for the means and machinations of their creation and the tricky details of their executive or legislative mandates.

More than that, they are now valuable to us for reasons rarely imagined by their founders and early champions. Everywhere in our perception of them, the neatness of some original idea of parks has been replaced by an ever-messier and hugely stimulating set of definitions and hopes. Even the two fundamental categories of sites to which our predecessors so fondly clung in discussing the park system—natural areas and cultural sites—are compromised by discomfiting realities. No site is purely one or the other. The grand old "nature parks" are under- and overlain with human culture, while the most urban cultural sites have echoes of the natural settings that preceded them, shaped them, and still influence them. The national park idea is a gloriously convoluted tangle of laws, theories, ideals, and dreams. Though it is the very complexity and administrative intractability of the system that makes it so good to think with, where should we begin to do that thinking? Where can we find some order, any order, that will help us make sense of it all?

Well, we have lots of places to look: in the laws and policies that 142 years of collective management of these places have given us; or rummaging around in our personal accumulation of facts, beliefs, values, and dreams; or in reading the best shots that generations of literary sages and visual artists have taken at sorting it out for themselves and thereby for us; or, perhaps best and deepest of all, in our own experiences in the parks. In considering past and future Yellowstones, it is with those experiences that I had better start.

There's a hill on the Blacktail Plateau in northern Yellowstone where for some years I frequently went, and for many more years I occasionally went, with my spotting scope. I was there to watch for bears, which meant that I was there especially to watch for elk, who were much better at watching for bears than I was.

On the hill, scanning the landscape, swatting mosquitoes, brushing off ticks, and dodging the occasional hailstorm, I was often reminded of something that the late Arnold Gingrich, founder of *Esquire* magazine, wrote about fishing: "So frequent the casts. So seldom a strike." Bear watching is, in that respect at least, a lot like fishing. You have your slow days and your fast days, but if you're doing it right you never have a bad day. A friend once told me that the bear's real gift to me was that it got me out there so I could soak up all the other things that are always going on. All I had to do was pay attention.

Since 1972, when I first worked in the park as a ranger-naturalist, I have always thought of myself as working for Yellowstone. Whoever I'm working for, year after year, I've taken part with many others in the century-plus holding action our society has waged over this park and its future. If you are interested in Yellowstone then you know that deciding its future is a source of endless controversy, emblematic of all the high-stakes debates over the public domain in the West. Most of us who are involved get pretty worked up about it. Several of its most intractable issues can make us despair that we will ever come to terms, ever agree on the best possible future Yellowstone.

That's why I went out to sit on my hill day after day to watch the elk watch for bears. That's why I waited for the bears to come. They did much more than distance me for a little while from all the contention and hostility that are a fact of life in Yellowstone's political realm. They reminded me what's behind all the fuss that makes it matter so much.

One summer evening about twenty-five years ago, I climbed the hill with two friends, Marilynn and Steve French. We set up our scopes and after watching that glorious landscape for a while and getting familiar with where the various groups of elk were grazing, Steve saw a big male grizzly bear. Those of you who know him can hear him say, "Thar's a griz."

This one, which we estimated at upwards of five hundred pounds, came into view near a forested slope of the Washburn Range about a mile and a half south of the hill.

Harsh evening light slanted across the plateau, etching long, sharp shadows from the clusters of burnt pine trees out across the meadows, and haloing the bear's dark brown coat in gold. The bear moved steadily to the northwest, angling across our field of view and, just by chance for half an hour or so, keeping roughly that same distance between himself and us. Now and then as he lifted a big forepaw from the short grass to take the next step, a shaft of sunlight hit just right and his long pale claws flashed like strobe lights, the only time I've ever seen this happen.

He stopped here and there to graze or dig for a few minutes, or to poke around in the higher brush—looking for newborn elk calves, which were abundant at the time—but then he moved on. Without seeming to notice, he flushed small bands of adult elk who shifted hastily out of his way as soon as they saw him approaching.

Thus without any violence or bluster, this one animal transformed fifty square miles of landscape. What had been an idyllic and even pastoral scene was abruptly changed into suspenseful, imminent drama. Sometimes the bear disappeared from our view when he dropped into a draw or passed through a dense stand of timber, but it didn't matter. Had this bear been utterly invisible, we still could have tracked his progress just by watching which elk were suddenly alert. The occasional synchronized aiming of a dozen elk noses pinpointed the bear almost as well as if he wore a bicycle pennant.

The light was failing, and we still had to hike back to the car, but we kept our eyes to our scopes as the bear marched diagonally across the low rolling hills to our west. As he made his way past a small grove of aspen, the bear suddenly looked to his right, and in three or four quick steps pounced and settled to his belly. In ragged unison, we said, "He got something."

At this distance in the gathering dark, we could not see what it was, but we agreed that it must be an elk calf. In that dim light, as the unmoving bear loafed over his dinner, our suspicions were confirmed. A cow elk appeared from a downslope fold in the landscape and made her way nervously toward the bear. Even in the low light, her concern was obvious as she edged closer and closer.

She finally got too close. The bear, just darker enough than the cow that we could barely make him out, must have risen a bit or even lunged at her, because she jumped back, then came in close again, then danced farther back to circle the meadow in agitation. Then darkness drove us from the hill.

I came back to the hill alone the next evening, and as I scanned the slopes and meadows with my scope, I saw a cow elk standing in that little grove of aspen, right where the bear had eaten the calf. She didn't move. She didn't even glance around, as cautious elk routinely do. She just stood there in the dusk, looking for all the world like she was waiting for something.

Standing Farther Back, and Then Further Back

Others who saw what we saw that evening would tell the story of the bear and the elk in their own unique ways, each piling on their own rendition of the interests and values that seem to be the special blessing and burden of our species. There is so much that must be thought. Every position has a counterposition, every question has an answer that is only another question in disguise. Had we just witnessed tragedy? loss? gain? beauty? wisdom? the past? the future? Was the bear the villain in this story? If you sided with the calf and cow, yes; but if later that summer you happened to see the adorable cubs fathered by that bear, maybe not. Was the cow grieving as she stood there the next night, or was she just absorbing some physiological shock of withdrawal from lactation? So many questions, so many layers of meaning just waiting to be explored. So many possible truths to be weighed. Welcome to the Yellowstone conversation.

I have stood with many people on the edge of wild settings watching life-and-death events: predations by bears, wolves, coyotes, foxes, trout, kingbirds, osprey, eagles; or the long, hard surrender of individual lives to winter, disease, and age; or the random casualties of accident and misjudgment; or just the abrupt expiration of each animal's personal lucky streak.

For some of my fellow observers, an almost motherly empathy ruled, and all they saw and felt was sorrow.

For others, the inevitability and necessity of death was the driving force that mattered more than the worth of any single life form, no matter how magnificent, beautiful, or cute.

For many if not most observers, our reaction was a swirl of conflicting feelings and ideas, a little of this and a little of that dragged out of the old conceptual hoard of emotion and intellect, then hastily stirred together, often leaving us at a loss, except a little breathless to have witnessed something so raw and authentic in a world where artificiality otherwise prevails. Empathy and exultation play out differently in each human heart. And whatever response we had, on a surprising number of occasions it involved tears.

Time was when the people who saw the lives of each individual wild animal in the most personal of terms seemed to occupy the moral high ground. After all, they were displaying the greatest sympathy for their fellow creatures, taking each lost baby bird and road-killed squirrel to heart like the death of a friend. The apparent heartlessness of *other* people, who placed some emotional distance or intellectual exercise between themselves and what Henry Beston called the "other nations," seemed cold, almost barbaric.

But the growing sophistication of our ecological awareness has redrawn this moral and ethical battlefield. New values, new beauties, have emerged. There are, indeed, ways to engage such scenes from other distances.

If you watch not the moment but the season, and see the entire elk herd straggle and pause for calving as they pursue the spring greenup across a wilderness landscape, you witness a wonder-filled natural pageant.

And if you stand back even further, you can reimagine the scene in terms of almost incomprehensible complexity—the interweavings of life and place not through a season but over decades, centuries, millennia. And from that distance, you witness yet another dance, perhaps the most elegant of all, as a place reshapes its inhabitants again and again and again—a dance whose rhythms you may only faintly discern when a single bear kills a single elk on a single day.

But there are yet other distances to be considered here. Century after century, as we have wondered and theorized over nature's spectacles, we have invariably put them to work in our hearts and our souls. In nature's doings we have found proof of God and proof of the needlessness of God— proof of the universe's perfect independence from any purpose, and proof of the universe's perfect sense—proof of our species' own innate centrality to all things, and proof of our species' utter meaninglessness. In the same natural scene we have at times found beauty, at other times evil. One generation's wasteland is the next generation's sublime. Nature is nothing if not malleable to our personal needs, and each of us will generally find what we are looking for out there.

But the important thing about nature, in fact the reason that wildness works for us at all, is that nature simply does not care what we find. Our experience, if it teaches us anything, teaches us that nature doesn't have a lot of use for answers, either about how it works or how we should feel about it. The answers are up to us.

The idea of Yellowstone is, like nature itself, a work in progress, a vast coming-to-terms that is all the more exciting and fulfilling for its daunting uncertainties. I love the learning that goes on out there, but I also have a hunch that we need the uncertainty just as much. It keeps us on our toes. Luckily, Yellowstone is very good at uncertainty.

I went to my hill to watch for elk who watched for bears because I *did* want to understand, but even more because what I found up there was perfect and beautiful and very powerful, and because it thrilled me to be drawn so irresistibly into the presence of such wildness. It would have been foolish to demand that my experiences settle anything, but somehow they always helped. Maybe that's asking enough.

Originals

I've worked hard to get to this point in my sense of what Yellowstone means to me. But I recognize that there are risks here. Those of us who are passionate about Yellowstone get pretty fond of ourselves. We revel in our sophisticated commitment to the place—in our awareness of the park's deepest magic. We are tempted to see ourselves as the end product of a long line of gradually less dumb people who didn't *get* Yellowstone quite as well as we do. Our condescension increases the further back we reach, all the way back to those well-intentioned but kind of dim characters who created the place in 1872 with only the vaguest clue to what they might have started.

Because condescending to our predecessors is nothing like the humility that we should be going on with in Yellowstone, I want to spend some time back then, when the Yellowstone conversation was new. The despair I have at times felt as a participant in Yellowstone's political, social, and scholarly skirmishes can hardly be compared to what the park's first friends must have felt back when it was desperately uncertain if a national park could even survive from one year to the next. In the park's first fifteen years of existence, it was subjected to a series of abuses with whose effects we are still living. The wholesale wildlife slaughter, rampant vandalism, concessioner malfeasance, and political corruption of those years were a model of Gilded Age disregard for the public good. And the disregard of the public for the park was nearly absolute.[1]

But just nearly. A small number of passionate and foresightful people saw in Yellowstone National Park great and previously unimagined things. They saw a future Yellowstone offering vital services to the American people and to the world—services far beyond the laudable but simple forms of "benefit and enjoyment" that were certainly intended by the act that created the park.

I'm not speaking here of the park's celebrated founders, those familiar heroes whose foresight we've praised so often, naming mountains after them just to be sure. I'm talking about a few of their contemporaries, people who looked harder at the park and became the first to wonder over the

deeper meanings of Yellowstone moments like the one that Marilynn and Steve and I witnessed that evening when a bear killed an elk.

Among the early champions of Yellowstone's deeper meanings, among the people who spoke of the park's great potential as a laboratory not just of science but of ideas, there is a mostly forgotten person we especially need to hear from first. His name was Theodore Comstock. A twenty-four-year-old Cornell-trained geologist, Comstock was just beginning a distinguished career in science, mining, and education when he explored Yellowstone's geological wonders as a member of the 1873 Jones Expedition.

Comstock's writings on Yellowstone National Park are a jolt to those of us who have become comfortable with the stereotype of Yellowstone's early defenders as well-meaning but fairly ignorant types who thought they were just creating an outdoor museum of weird geology, or a great tourist attraction.

The jarring historical reality is that Theodore Comstock often sounds remarkably like us. For one thing, he was quite willing to link the name of Yellowstone with another globally important name of his day—Charles Darwin.

Imagine what it would have been like for Comstock and his contemporaries, working in the earth sciences when Darwin's milestone books *On the Origin of Species* (1859) and *The Descent of Man* (1871) were essentially current events. The sixth edition of *On the Origin of Species*, Darwin's final revision, appeared the same year that the park was created. The scientific world, and indeed the public, was caught up in an ever-widening debate over the ideas of Darwin and his predecessors and—as time has passed ever *since* Darwin—over the bewildering array of alternative ideas proposed by Darwin's various detractors and supporters. This growing intellectual turmoil was clearly on Comstock's mind as he described what he saw as the highest possible use of Yellowstone National Park.

The text by Comstock that I'm going to quote here appeared in *The American Naturalist* in February and March 1874. Already in 1874, out there in the park, things were going seriously wrong at the hands of careless tourists, vandals, market hunters, and an oblivious Congress. In the minds of most of the people who gave it any thought, Yellowstone was probably destined eventually to become a vast Saratoga-style resort. But in the minds and hearts of a few hopeful people like Comstock, a much more challenging future Yellowstone was already under construction.

Most of all, Comstock, like a few of his contemporaries, was profoundly enthusiastic about the opportunities presented by Yellowstone for pathbreaking science.[2] He saw in the park "fresh matter for research in nearly every department of science."[3] Aside from the obvious geological appeal of the place, he championed the study of *all* the life in the park, and he paid special attention to the large mammals and urged that all the large mammals of the West be preserved in Yellowstone National Park.[4] In fact, Comstock asserted that if an important western species didn't happen to be in the park, then someone should go get some and put them there![5]

This is a fascinating comment. We must read Comstock carefully here, for he wrote at a formative stage in the development of the national park idea. Philosophically and in their formal policies, American national parks abandoned the idea of introducing nonnative species early in the twentieth century. Since then, protection of native life forms has been a fundamental mission of the parks, as has exclusion of nonnative species and suppression or removal of those already in the park. But perhaps the most curious thing about Comstock's suggestion is that the only animal that he specifically named as needing to be brought to the park was the bison. He apparently assumed that bison did not inhabit the park because he did not see them during his visit. They were there; earlier visitors, as well as other visitors at the time of his visit, did see them, including fellow members of his own party, who happened to travel a different route than he did.[6]

I mention Comstock's enthusiasm for introducing new species of animals to the park as a cautionary note. We are not careful with history. In the heat of our need for reinforcement of our beliefs, we tend to bypass the nuances of our ancestors' statements. We like to wander up and down the aisles of the Great Historical Quotation Costco and shop for user-friendly pronouncements and tasty aphorisms that will make us feel good about what we've already decided. In our need for historical validation, we choose our prophets retroactively, picking the voices and phrases that suit. Comstock was a smart and extraordinarily foresightful man, but he inhabited a world different from ours, and deserves not to be oversimplified. Such are the perils of historical hero worship.

With that caution in mind, today what we see as most significant about Comstock's recommendation is *why* he wanted to make sure that the native western wildlife species were all saved in the park. It wasn't just that he wanted to use Yellowstone National Park as a place to stockpile vanishing wildlife, like a big drive-through zoo. Here is what Comstock said:

> Momentous questions are now agitating the scientific world, calling for experiment and observation which are daily becoming less possible, owing in a great measure to the obliterating influence of modern civilization. Thus it would almost seem that the present difficulties in the way of the solution of many questions, bearing upon the process of natural selection, will soon become insurmountable if some means are not employed to render more practicable the study of animals in a state of nature.
>
> I have not space to treat this subject as it deserves, but for this and other reasons, I desire to call attention to what appears to me one of the most important uses to which the park can be put, viz.: *the preservation from extinction of at least the characteristic mammals and birds of the west, as far as they can be domiciled in this section.*[7]

Two points jump out here. The first is that Comstock recognized that as the planet's wild places diminished, we were running out of places where, as he put it, "the process of natural selection" could still function. He was, in fact, proposing that Yellowstone National Park should become an evolutionary observatory. He wanted the park kept as wild as possible for the sake of what it could contribute to the scientific dialogue. In short, Comstock aimed to put Yellowstone center stage in the planet's foremost intellectual drama—which is precisely where many of us agree it should be today. He hitched Yellowstone to some of the most demanding scientific questions of his time—and of ours.

But in that same quotation, Comstock brought up a second touchy subject, that of extinction. Again, think of his times. It had only been in the late 1700s that even the *possibility* of extinction was first seriously confronted in the scientific literature.[8] But by Comstock's time, the swiftly accumulating fossil record had established that many animals had indeed disappeared during the earth's long history, a history that presented a fabulous chronicle of biological change over immense stretches of time. And, as Comstock saw it, humans were causing just such changes in the American West. In his urgent words, "unless prompt and vigorous measures are instituted to check the wholesale slaughter now in progress in our western wilds, the *zoölogical record of to-day must rapidly pass into the domain of the paleontologist.*"[9]

Having defined the park's higher role this way, he then reinforced the
point that this should be about *all* the wild western animals—Yellowstone
should serve to save all the parts, as someone would so famously say many
years later. Most notably, Comstock explicitly included in this appeal the
large carnivores that were at that time pretty much without friends throughout the West.[10]

It's especially interesting how he defended this recommendation. We
might have expected him to point out that natural selection, the preservation
of which he explicitly championed in Yellowstone, couldn't function without
all the factors that might influence it, including predation, but it isn't even
clear from his comments how well he understood that. Instead, he concen-
trated on allaying fears about the risks of having all these big carnivores wan-
dering around loose in a park full of tourists. To allay those fears, he went
against the almost universal popular and scientific opinion of his time, again
sounding quite modern, saying that if we behaved ourselves around the big
carnivores, they really weren't that dangerous. Here is how he put it:

> I make this statement advisedly, for, although I have repeatedly
> been exposed to attacks from predatory animals in this country
> and in Brazil, including the black, cinnamon, and grizzly bears,
> the puma, jaguar, wolverine and wolf, and even the venomous
> reptiles such as the rattlesnake and the boa, I have always found
> them ready to run at my approach.[11]

He knew what he was up against in bucking public opinion:

> I am aware that my ideas upon this subject are quite novel to
> many, but I believe them to be supported by the facts, as well as
> by the testimony of experience. My own observation, by itself, is
> of little value, but I have based my conclusions very largely upon
> the evidence of those whose wide knowledge of the habits of these
> animals in a state of nature best qualifies them to judge.[12]

It is still an uphill battle to convince a lot of people that Comstock was
on the right track with his "quite novel" ideas. I wish I could send him a can
of bear spray.

Having made these breathtakingly comprehensive appeals for preserving
a remarkably modern version of ecological wholeness in Yellowstone, Comstock went on. In a statement that seems prescient to the point of scariness,
he identified an extraordinary but, at that time, little noticed park feature
that would remain uncelebrated for another century. He said:

There is one young but active science—microscopy—which has as yet scarcely entered this field, but which, I firmly believe, will discover within the limits of the Park most valuable treasures. The act of Congress providing for this reservation insures the preservation of the greater portion of whatever may be available for this purpose.

Among the most interesting objects for the microscope, will be found the colloidal and filamentous products of the hot springs, the minute vegetable and animal life of both hot and cold springs, the animal and vegetable parasites, and the numerous crystalline deposits of the hot springs and geysers.[13]

Modern research in the realms of the "microscopy" to which Comstock referred have surely fulfilled any promise he may have seen in them. Modern microbiological research in Yellowstone National Park has changed our lives. It has ranged from (again with the Darwinian undercurrents) origins-of-life questions to (and again) fundamental matters of the biological identity of humans. Many of us have followed the politically, scientifically, and legally messy saga of modern bioprospecting in the parks, an arena in which native microorganisms, having long thrived anonymously in Yellowstone's thermal features, are now of intense commercial interest. We can only nod our heads and wonder what other "most valuable treasures" predicted by Comstock remain undiscovered, and how we will deal with them.

Comstock's explicit encouragement of evolutionary thinking as a management tool for future Yellowstone should do more than raise our opinion of our predecessors in deliberations over the park's purpose and fate. Perhaps it is time to recast our notion of Yellowstone at least a bit, and recognize that from the beginning its fate has been entwined in the scientific revolution that has raged since the park was created. And once we start looking at Yellowstone as part of the theater of Darwinism, other historical elements begin to shift as well.

Rocks, and a Single Rock

It was no mere happenstance that it was a geologist, not a biologist, who first so clearly articulated Yellowstone's vital potential role in the future of natural history and the biological sciences, though I confess that it took me too long to understand what the geologists were up to back then. Forty years ago, when I first began to explore the publications of Yellowstone's pioneering scientific survey parties, I was disappointed and puzzled to see that so much of their time and attention went to geology and paleontology, and so little to the wondrous array of plants and animals that were glorifying the park with their presence while these scientists were pecking away at rocks and hot spring deposits with their little hammers. Most puzzling of all was the almost complete lack of scientific attention given to what we now think of as the "glamor animals"—the large mammals whose doings consume so much of our interest and energy today. The first explorer-scientists even paid more attention to the invertebrates. What was the problem?

The problem, of course, was me presuming that their interests in the 1870s should be the same as ours today. Wildlife, ephemeral on the landscape, was a relatively minor concern of people who, for several reasons including the effects of the furor over Darwin's work, had much bigger scientific game in their sights. Besides, when that first generation of scientific explorers came to the park, the wildlife wasn't even a primary attraction of Yellowstone National Park except to the extent that its meat might feed their party.[14] Until 1883, when controversy over the horrible slaughter of park animals by market hunters finally did reach critical mass and hunting was made illegal in the park, wildlife were treated as thoughtlessly and wastefully as they were elsewhere in the wide open West. (Once wildlife became an officially sanctioned attraction of the park, they consumed progressively more and more of managers' attention and came to dominate that attention very quickly.)

But fossils! In Comstock's time, fossils were a big scientific deal. They provided essential information and, handled right by an ambitious scientist, they were much more likely to promise professional glory than the most spectacular live wild animals could.

That said, I still have felt a little vindicated lately to notice that the heavy focus on fossil hunting among these early government-sponsored expeditions may have raised some eyebrows even back then. In his 1879 annual report, Ferdinand Hayden, the foremost scientific investigator in early Yellowstone history, apparently felt compelled to justify all the time his crews spent studying fossils. He explained why fossils were so important to the great government surveys throughout the West:

> By examining the publications of the survey, it will be seen that much attention has been given to the ancient fauna and flora of our Western Territories. The memoirs by Leidy, Cope, Lesquereux, Scudder, Meek, and White will always remain as imperishable monuments of their labors in their respective departments. The value of their studies in connection with geological explorations and surveys is often in danger of being underestimated by not being correctly understood; but the importance of such work may be indicated by the fact that it is upon the study of fossil remains that the whole system of geology was originally based, and which study now forms the only reliable foundation for the correct classification of the stratified rocks of the earth.
>
> The study of the fossil remains of animals and plants not only adds immensely to the sciences of zoology and botany, giving them a completeness which could never be attained by the study of the living forms alone, but it has immediate and direct practical application in the elucidation of the systematic geology of every region as well as a general and universal classification of the stratified rocks.

In other words, fossils were studied so intensively because they were the key to reading the rocks (today we often refer to them as "index fossils"). The fossil species that appeared in a given strata were vital tools for dating the rock itself, and thus for creating the geological biography of each region studied. And, as Hayden said in what seems to be an implicit bow toward evolutionary science, the "completeness" of our understanding of the present animal life—the "living forms"—of a region is mightily enriched by discovering their fossil predecessors.[15]

Comstock's and Hayden's perspectives are interesting in the greater context of American science at the time, for they demonstrate that the post–Civil War scientist-explorers had a dramatically different view of government survey work in the West than was held by the previous generation. In his magnificent *Exploration and Empire: The Explorer and the Scientist in the Winning of the American West*, historian William Goetzmann characterized the interests and disinterests of scientific researchers who participated in the earlier "Great Western Reconnaissance"[16] in the two decades before the Civil War:

> There was, of course, not a hint of Darwinian speculation or even of evolution in general. There had been no interest in such questions on the part of the Americans, who were bent on description and classification. Likewise, the explorer-scientists, and their Washington partners, had very little, if any, idea of ecology or the relationship of birds and animals to their environment and the corresponding life and food cycle. Unlike similar ventures among whalers on the high seas, where the routes and migrations of the great mammals were carefully studied, no one concerned himself with the habits of the buffalo and other wild game. Even the beaver was largely ignored, as were the migratory fowl. In short, there was no attempt at all to relate animals and men on any level— either in the Darwinian realm of evolution or in the practical realm of human and animal ecology.[17]

Thus Comstock, and to varying degrees a number of his contemporaries, displayed a very different view of life than had their scientific predecessors in the American West. As reflected in their areas of concentration as researchers, Comstock's generation cared very much about the issues of evolution and ecology, and applied their growing awareness of both to the landscapes and native species they studied. That awareness would be brought to constructive fruition by a young contemporary of theirs who, inspired and alarmed by the message he read in the West's beds of ancient bones, would contribute more than anyone else of his day to laying the groundwork for the reserve of wildness that Yellowstone National Park eventually became. His name was George Bird Grinnell.

In 1870, Yale University's original paleontology professor, Othniel C. Marsh, came west on the second of the fossil-hunting expeditions that would eventually earn him scientific accolades, including the praise of Charles Darwin, who regarded Marsh's work on the fossil horses of western North America as an important exemplar of Darwin's theories in *On the Origin of Species*.[18] On that 1870 expedition, Marsh had in tow a small but eager band of Yale undergraduates, including twenty-year-old Grinnell. Though Grinnell's father dreamed that his son would join him in the family brokerage firm, Grinnell had been well primed for the study of nature by a childhood that included frequent neighborly acquaintance with the widow and two sons of John James Audubon. He was a passionate naturalist and sportsman, ripe for the unforgettable experiences with western wildlife and native cultures that Marsh's expedition provided.

Grinnell biographer Michael Punke says that Grinnell's "adventures with the Marsh expedition represented the most important formative events of his life."[19] Grinnell authority John Reiger elaborated on what those formative events amounted to: it was thanks to Marsh that "Grinnell was in the vanguard of the ascending generation of more sophisticated explorers, and his awareness of the great transformations the earth had undergone made him recognize that the land was not invulnerable as most of his contemporaries seemed to believe. His study of fossil animals taught him that the long-term survival of a species was the exception, not the rule."[20] During that first western trip Grinnell witnessed the ongoing overkill of wildlife that careful observers were already saying would lead to the annihilation of not just the animals but the way of life they represented—both to the native people who had lived with the animals for thousands of years and to the newcomers like Grinnell, who felt they were discovering the West's wilderness wonders only in time to see them vanish.

Like Comstock, Grinnell was shocked into action by the prospect of the animals' extinction, and like Comstock, Yellowstone became a focal point of his reaction. First visiting the park in 1875 as a zoologist for the Ludlow expedition, he made some of the first professional zoological collections since the park's establishment. He immediately saw what the unfunded, unprotected, and unappreciated park was up against.

But unlike Comstock, Grinnell devoted the rest of his personal and professional life to conservation causes, among which Yellowstone was always a high priority. A prolific writer in several fields, by the late 1870s he was a columnist for the influential outdoor periodical *Forest and Stream*. By 1880 he owned *Forest and Stream* and spent the next thirty-one years as its editor, publishing hundreds of items about Yellowstone—everything from short notes, to letters from informed local correspondents, to major feature articles by journalists who visited the park on *Forest and Stream* assignments. Through those articles and his other work, including as cofounder with Theodore Roosevelt of the Boone and Crockett Club (1887), he popularized what we would now call ecosystem-scale thinking, fostering in the growing conservation movement recognition of Yellowstone National Park as a terrific opportunity to set a new standard for intelligent management of wild settings.

In that effort, Grinnell taught his readers to reimagine the park (as was being done for the Adirondacks in upstate New York) as a great natural water reservoir: as long as the park's forests remained uncut, they would moderate the flow of water in the various river systems whose headwaters

were in or near the park, to the perpetual benefit of society, industry, and agriculture in all directions downhill and downstream from Yellowstone. He likewise convinced sportsmen that closing the park to sport hunting in 1883 was a great idea. He taught them to imagine the park as a wildlife "reservoir" that, as long as the park's calving grounds were protected, would perpetually provide surrounding lands with annual seasonal migrations of animals to be hunted for sport and food.[21]

In these and other ways, Grinnell championed Yellowstone as a functioning wildland, an essential tool in the battle against extinction. In the face of the headlong development and alteration of other western lands, Grinnell said, "There is one spot left, a single rock about which this tide will break, and past which it will sweep, leaving it undefiled by the unsightly traces of civilization. Here in this Yellowstone Park the wild game of the West may be preserved from extermination." A century before the modern "Greater Yellowstone" movement finally captured our imagination, Grinnell and a few like-minded hopefuls campaigned tirelessly for the enlargement and realignment of the park's boundaries, better to reflect ecological realities and the needs of its native inhabitants. He sought in many ways to bring to reality Comstock's dream of a Yellowstone dedicated to the preservation not only of wild things but of wildness itself—not just the parts, but the process.

Theodore Comstock stands tall at one end of a long and convoluted thread in national park history, a thread that thickened as it wove through the work of many other very smart and far-seeing people, from Comstock and his contemporaries, including Grinnell, to early twentieth-century thinkers Joseph Grinnell, Charles Adams, and George Melendez Wright, to the amazing array of people studying the park today.[22] These were—and are—people who even among themselves often don't agree about what would be the best possible future Yellowstone, but who inspire us with their conviction that we must never settle for anything less.

Science is central to this enterprise because scientific advances in our understanding of how Yellowstone works are at the heart of how the park is interpreted and enjoyed by all of us today. By giving us a stronger grasp of how nature works, and by thus opening new avenues of thought about matters of authenticity, wildness, and even aesthetics, science has reshaped not just management but the public's idea of what to enjoy about a wild place, and how to go about enjoying it.[23] For me, without science's lessons in how wildness works, watching that bear kill that elk calf on Blacktail Plateau would have been a very different and far less fulfilling experience. For many of us, the very beauty we find in wild nature has become dependent upon science to tease out the fullness of wonder that nature can provide.[24]

With hindsight, we can look back on the whole long Yellowstone conversation and see the historic effect of this thread—of all this watching, thinking, researching, debating, legislating. In many ways Yellowstone has slowly trended toward the values that Comstock and his fellow early visionaries had in mind for the best future Yellowstone. Nature gradually was given more room to make its own decisions. Saratoga gradually receded as an option. Whatever Comstock, Grinnell, and their friends might think of what we have made of Yellowstone, I like to believe that they would be gratified to read this statement in the National Park Service's current *Management Policies*: "The Service recognizes that natural processes and species are evolving, and the Service will allow this evolution to continue—minimally influenced by human actions."[25]

RESULTS

On any given day, this business of trying to get Yellowstone right can be very hard to watch. The crowds and traffic are oppressive; the bureaucracies lurch along at fits and starts; the advocacy rhetoric seems only to grow more shrill; ecological process constantly bumps political boundaries; the scientists disagree among themselves about ever more complex findings; someone is *always* fishing in my favorite spot; and every little bit of progress, at least as we define progress today, seems to take for*ever.*

But somehow there are results. Each result comes with exasperating compromises, but it's been a long time since anyone with much sense said that this was going to be easy, or that we would ever be satisfied. Personally, I have no intention of ever being satisfied, but I have to admit that we have gotten a lot better at doing Yellowstone than we were in those first decades, when Comstock and his type were widely ignored voices in the wilderness—and we didn't even know if Yellowstone would last.

Standing back for a better look, we can see these good results. These are things we should keep in mind for the sake of our perspective: the human footprint on the landscape of Yellowstone National Park probably peaked before 1920, and has declined substantially since then. Public road mileage probably peaked by the 1940s and has declined significantly since. Native people have a historically unprecedented level of enfranchisement in park management deliberations. Women can and regularly do hold top positions in the Yellowstone work force. Science is now, finally, a required component of management decision making, and scientists are no longer perceived by managers as just another special-interest group. Hot springs are no longer plumbed for swimming pools and hotel bathtubs. The park's various small zoos are gone. The garbage dumps are gone. Wolves and mountain lions are back. Coyotes and raptors that were once shot on sight now have first-class citizenship. Fire does what fire is supposed to do.

These results may seem to us to have taken a lot longer than they should have, but we should not treat them lightly, for they are monumental gains. I guarantee you that they were neither easy nor inevitable.[26]

What's more, some stunning potential mistakes have been fought off so successfully that most people don't even know they were once serious issues, and in some cases nearly became real. Here are a few items from a chilling list of Yellowstone's historical "almosts": the Yellowstone National Park Railroad, with stations at all major attractions and spur lines to all entrances, the Bechler water reservoir system, the Grand Loop Monorail, the Bighorn Pass Road, the Yellowstone Lake outlet dam, the elevator to the bottom of the canyon at the Lower Falls, the water diversion tunnel from Yellowstone Lake to Shoshone Lake to Henrys Fork, and the Thorofare Road. Imagine any of those happening. Imagine them all.

It is difficult to make quantitative or qualitative comparisons of anxiety levels across generations, but it is at least as true today as it was in Theodore Comstock's time that, as he put it, "momentous questions are now agitating the scientific world, calling for experiment and observation which are daily becoming less possible, owing in a great measure to the obliterating influence of modern civilization." Each generation is agitated by its own share of momentous questions. Yellowstone regularly makes us feel, as historian

Aubrey Haines said in describing the park's management challenges nearly half a century ago, that we stand "at a crossroad, faced by fearful decisions."[27] In defining the next future Yellowstone, there are always crossroads, always fearful decisions. The more we know about the place, the more we love it, but the more we know, the more things we find to be alarmed about. Our alarm is genuine, and is often fully justified. Crisis is nearly a steady state.

And I must tell you that in the history of the national parks, crisis is the highest form of peril. Crisis loosens *all* the cannons. Crisis, by its very nature and by the tone of its times, stirs panic and generates a vague but mighty need for urgent action if not desperate measures. That's not necessarily a bad thing, as long as we keep in mind that for the wise and crafty among us, crisis is also a rarified form of opportunity, when all stakeholders proclaim that their standing agendas are precisely the answer.

So pick a Yellowstone issue that is widely regarded as a crisis. Climate change; bison population increases; elk population declines; aging infrastructure; aging visitation; invasive organisms from all corners of creation. How are we going to deal with these things?

Well, we will deal with them through the same ponderous exercise of debate, research, hand-wringing, politics, law, policy, and hard work that we have as we conducted many previous such exercises. And the more I watch Yellowstone, the more I begrudgingly respect that process. It always takes too long to suit me, but it also slows down the conversation and compels us to listen to each other. It saves us from mistakes of haste and impulse, and makes it harder for any one interest to run away with the process.[28]

Having already expressed my skepticism about the way we tend to use history, I will now resort to history myself, because I think that in the urgency of each crisis we can forget, as Theodore Comstock and Aubrey Haines both reminded us, that however dire the *crisis du jour* may seem, we've been here before.

Here is the case I've been making lately when I try to think about Yellowstone's more or less permanent state of crisis. In the following list of sweeping historical generalizations, when I say "we" I refer to the entire Yellowstone community, including managers, academics, advocacy groups, casual visitors, legislators, and anyone else who cares about the future of Yellowstone.[29]

First, since 1872, every generation of us who cares about Yellowstone has been composed mostly of people who were reasonably certain what the best future Yellowstone should be like.

Second, at least in the judgment of later generations, they were wrong.

Third, every generation has had to make its own fearful decisions without enough information. Often, they didn't even know they *needed* more information.

Fourth, in our confidence about what Yellowstone needs, we have regularly sold nature short—underestimating its power, its resilience, its complexity, and its capacity to surprise us with unimagined consequences of our well-intentioned attempts to do right by it.

Fifth, learning about what Comstock called the "state of nature" continues to prove itself worthy of being a, if not the, fundamental purpose of Yellowstone, and we always learn less when we interfere with that state, no matter how pure our intentions.

Last, the decisions of our predecessors that we most appreciate are the ones that don't limit our options today. We are constantly telling ourselves that we are saving national parks for future generations. But at the same time we don't dare lock our descendants too tightly into decisions based on our beliefs and values. Part of what we must save for future generations is choices.

The exciting rate at which we are still discovering more of Theodore Comstock's "most valuable treasures" in Yellowstone suggests that we still have a lot to learn. We have not arrived at a finished idea of Yellowstone. We are not at the other end of a process that began with Comstock; with luck, we're not even in the middle. The process can go on forever unless we lose interest. And that would be the worst betrayal of any future Yellowstone that I can imagine.

It amazes me that it has already been nearly twenty years since the wolves were brought back and set off a whole new round of changes in our search for our preferred future Yellowstone. From whatever distance we watch, we can see how wolves affect those changes—everything from changes in the balance of political power among Yellowstone's constituencies, to changes in the scientific dialogues about the park's ecological community, to changes in regional tourism promotion and merchandising. Whatever place we occupy on the spectrum of opinions about wolves, we sense these changes and wonder how they reflect on our own interests.

Wolves have shown us that we are still putting Yellowstone together in our heads and hearts, still standing off at some unaccustomed distance, hoping to get that better, clearer, more satisfying look that we know is out there somewhere, if only we can find the right place to stand.

There was a morning in the Lamar Valley, not long after the wolves had arrived. As the word got out how easy and exciting it was to see these animals, the roadside crowds grew quickly. A new Yellowstone constituency emerged and began to stretch its economic and political muscles. Through dumb luck, my timing had been great; I'd spent the previous few years out there watching how things worked, and now I'd get to see how things worked with this dramatic new player on the field. Things were changing again, and after a while I began to realize that I was going out there to witness the changes as well as to continue enjoying wild Yellowstone.

This day, I stood by the road at one end of a line of eager new wolf watchers. Their scopes and binoculars were aimed expectantly in various directions as they tried to find their Holy Grail out there, somewhere.

After a while, there was a stir among the watchers just a few scopes down the row from me, as a sharp-eyed observer picked something out of the rocky terrain a couple miles off on a high slope. The instant of breath-holding excitement was palpable, but it was followed by the astonishing and wondrous remark: "Nah, it's just a grizzly bear."

NOTES

1. General historical information that I invoke or summarize in this paper is available in great detail in Aubrey Haines, *The Yellowstone Story,* volumes 1 and 2 (Boulder: Colorado Associated University Press and the Yellowstone Library and Museum Association, 1977), and Paul Schullery, *Searching for Yellowstone: Ecology and Wonder in the Last Wilderness* (Boston: Houghton Mifflin, 1997).

2. Comstock was not first to celebrate Yellowstone National Park's scientific potential. Other champions of the park as a unique scientific opportunity included Lt. Gustavus Doane who, in his official report on his 1870 visit to the area (even before it was made a park) as part of the famed Washburn-Langford-Doane Expedition, concluded that "as a field for scientific research, it promises great results; in the branches of geology, mineralogy, botany, zoology, and ornithology it is probably the greatest laboratory that nature furnishes on the surface of the globe." Gustavus Doane, *Report of Lieutenant Gustavus C. Doane upon the So-called Yellowstone Expedition of 1870* (Washington, DC: U.S. Government Printing Office, 41st Cong., 3d Sess.; Senate Exec. Doc. 51, 1871), 37–38. These sentiments were echoed and elaborated on by geologist Ferdinand Hayden, whose scientific surveys of the Yellowstone area in 1871, 1872, and 1878 inspired him to become the best-known early proponent of Yellowstone science.

3. Theodore Comstock, "The Yellowstone National Park I: Its Scientific Value," *The American Naturalist* 8, no. 2 (February 1874): 71.

4. Comstock's discussion of this matter is somewhat convoluted but it is necessary to sort it out. In "The Yellowstone National Park I," 72–76, Comstock provided, by a combination of narrative in the text and a partial species list in a footnote, an inventory of the mammal species that he knew to exist in "the west," which he did not define precisely but that seemed to include the Rocky Mountains. Thus, the narrative included the following large mammals: bison; wolverine; grizzly bear; beaver; a hare species; moose; "blacktail," "cotton tailed," and "mule deer"; "prong-horn antelope"; "the mountain sheep or big horn"; and reference to other smaller mammals. Then, in the footnote that followed this portion of the narrative, Comstock provided a "partial list" that "comprises only the more important of the mammals and

birds observed by myself during the past summer (exclusive of those already mentioned), with some few additions from the report of Mr. C. H. Merriam, Zoologist of the Snake River Division of Dr. Hayden's expedition of 1872, in order to include a portion of the fauna of Idaho and Montana."

I assume that Comstock intended that his readers were meant to combine the species named in the narrative with those listed in the footnote in order to have a reasonably complete list of the animals he was concerned with.

5. In the second part of his article, "The Yellowstone National Park II: Its Improvement," *The American Naturalist* 8, no. 3 (March 1874): 163, Comstock explained that "not all the forms included in my list are representatives of the park fauna." Because he used the plural, i.e., "forms," I assume that there was more than one species that he believed must be brought into the park, but (in the third footnote, same page) he named only bison, calling it a "foreign" species because it is "not now found within the limits of the reserved tract." Another reason that Comstock's characterization of bison as "foreign" to Yellowstone National Park is odd is that he left two separate accounts of seeing bison bones in the park. In "The Yellowstone National Park II," 163, third footnote, he spoke of bison bones, specifically the "abundant remains which are now bleaching in the valleys both within and adjacent to the park, showing that they have but recently been driven from these haunts." And in Theodore Comstock, "Geological report," in W. A. Jones, *Report upon the reconnaissance of northwestern Wyoming including Yellowstone National Park, made in the summer of 1873* (Washington, DC: U.S. Government Printing Office), 213, he described finding "the skull and other bones of a bison" in a small cave near Mammoth Hot Springs.

I conclude from these statements by Comstock that he assumed that bison had but recently been eradicated or, as he put it, "driven from these haunts." Thus in modern parlance we would say that what Comstock was really recommending was not the *introduction* of bison into Yellowstone National Park, but their *restoration*.

However, an important question about his intentions remains. In "The Yellowstone National Park II," 163, footnote 2, he said, "Besides the animals referred to, it seems to me quite possible to domicile in this region, a few at least of those species of other fauna which are in danger of rapid extermination; at any rate, experiments of this nature could do no harm, and they might often prove very beneficial." Was this a suggestion to import into Yellowstone National Park animal species from beyond the native western fauna?

6. Comstock's colleague, topographer Paul LeHardy, left a manuscript autobiography that included an account of this 1873 visit to the park. In that document, LeHardy reported that he and a companion visited the present Lamar Valley, where they "saw quite a number of Buffalo." Paul LeHardy,

"Autobiography of Paul LeHardy, surveyor and map maker, covering in full, his personal experiences and observations while with the 1873 expedition into the Yellowstone Plateau under Captain W. A. Jones." Typescript by his son, 1961. Copy in Yellowstone National Park Research Library, Manuscript file, Yellowstone National Park, Wyoming, 101. Apparently LeHardy did not share this information with Comstock.

7. Comstock, "The Yellowstone National Park I," 72.

8. Stephen Jay Gould, *The Structure of Evolutionary Theory* (Cambridge, MA: Belknap Press of Harvard University Press, 2002), 486.

9. Comstock, "The Yellowstone National Park I," 72–73, emphasis in original.

10. Ibid., 75–76.

11. Ibid., 76, first footnote. Boa constrictors are not venomous.

12. Ibid., 76, second footnote. I dearly wish he had given us the names of a few of "those whose wide knowledge of the habits of these animals" whose opinions he had sought. They certainly weren't numerous among the mainstream writers on western carnivores in the popular press in the 1870s.

13. Ibid., 78.

14. For an overview of the early development of wildlife protection in the park, and its rise as an actual wildlife reserve, see Schullery, *Searching for Yellowstone*, 68–88, 108–27.

15. Mike Foster, in his biography of Hayden, *Strange Genius: The Life of Ferdinand Vandeveer Hayden* (Niwot, CO: Roberts Rinehart Publishers, 1994), 110, 121–23, 189–92, and 197, makes the intriguing point that though Hayden had a keen awareness of Darwin's works and the debates over evolution, and though his own geological surveys were generating significant new fossil findings, he chose not to engage the controversial topic of evolution directly in his publications. Comstock was, in that respect, more willing to go out on a limb in a scientific community in which many were still skeptical of, if not actively opposed to, Darwin's views. It is a matter of more than slight interest in this respect that in 1859, on a much earlier western expedition, Hayden was probably the first scientist to discover a North American dinosaur fossil.

16. William H. Goetzmann, *Exploration and Empire: The Explorer and the Scientist in the Winning of the American West* (Austin: Texas State Historical Association, 1993), 302.

17. Ibid., 323–24.

18. Ibid., 425.

19. Michael Punke, *Last Stand: George Bird Grinnell, the Battle to Save the Buffalo, and the Birth of the New West* (New York: Smithsonian Books/HarperCollins Publishers, 2007), 26.

20. John Reiger, ed., *The Passing of the Great West: Selected Papers of George Bird Grinnell* (New York: Charles Scribner, 1972), 55.

21. For more on Grinnell and Yellowstone in addition to Punke, *Last Stand*, and Reiger, *The Passing of the Great West*, see John Reiger, *American Sportsmen and the Origins of Conservation* (Corvallis: Oregon State University Press, 2001), and Sarah Broadbent, "Sportsmen and the Evolution of the Conservation Idea in Yellowstone: 1882–1894," M.A. Thesis, Montana State University, Bozeman, 1997.

22. The development of ecological thinking as an element of Yellowstone National Park management in the twentieth century is best described in James Pritchard, *Preserving Yellowstone's Natural Conditions: Science and the Perception of Nature* (Lincoln: University of Nebraska Press, 1999).

23. I have explored the influence of scientific research findings on the aesthetics of nature appreciation briefly in Paul Schullery, "Greater Yellowstone Science: Past, Present, and Future," *Yellowstone Science* 18, no. 2 (2010): 11–13.

24. See also my comments on the relationship between science and the changing idea of natural beauty in Ken Burns and Dayton Duncan, *The National Parks: America's Best Idea* (New York: Alfred A. Knopf, 2009), 252–55.

25. National Park Service, U.S. Department of the Interior, Management Policies 2006: The Guide to Managing the National Park System; 4. Natural Resource Management, Introduction, paragraph 1, http://www.nps.gov/policy/mp/policies.html.

26. Two works that document these gains in considerable detail are Aubrey Haines, *The Yellowstone Story*, volumes 1 and 2, and Paul Schullery, *Searching for Yellowstone*.

27. Haines, *The Yellowstone Story*, volume 2, 386.

28. An essential and penetrating analysis of the process by which results are gotten or missed in the ongoing evolution of Yellowstone National Park management is Michael Yochim, *Protecting Yellowstone: Science and the Politics of National Park Management* (Albuquerque: University of New Mexico Press, 2013).

29. Some of the ideas expressed here are developed in greater detail in the publications that follow: Paul Schullery, "Greater Yellowstone Science: Past, Present, and Future"; "Sort of a Historian: Paul Schullery Retires," *Yellowstone Science* 17, no. 3 (2009), esp. 17–18; and Paul Schullery, "The Narratives of Yellowstone," Aubrey Haines Lecture, presented at the Eleventh Biennial Scientific Conference on the Greater Yellowstone Ecosystem, Mammoth Hot Springs Hotel, Yellowstone National Park, October 10, 2012. In press, *Yellowstone Science*.

About the Author

Paul Schullery began his conservation career in 1972 as a ranger-naturalist in Yellowstone National Park and has held several other positions in the park, including historian-archivist, chief of cultural resources, and senior editor in the Yellowstone Center for Resources. He is the author, coauthor, or editor of more than forty books, including *Mountain Time* (1984); *Searching for Yellowstone* (1997); *Lewis and Clark Among the Grizzlies* (2002); *Myth and History in the Creation of Yellowstone National Park* (with Lee Whittlesey, 2003); and *This High, Wild Country* (2010).

For his work as a writer, historian, and conservationist, Paul has received honorary doctorates of letters from Montana State University (1997) and Ohio University (2013); the Wallace Stegner Award from the University of Colorado Center for the American West (1998); a Panda Award from Wildscreen International (2002) for his script for the ABC/PBS film *Yellowstone: America's Sacred Wilderness*; the Communications Leadership Award (2008) from the U.S. Interagency Grizzly Bear Committee for his "extraordinary work on grizzly bear recovery"; and the Communications Award from the George Wright Society (2011) for his "outstanding contributions to conservation history, national park policy, and the understanding of wildlife."

Paul was an advisor and interviewee for the Ken Burns film *The National Parks* (2009). He is currently Scholar-in-Residence at the Montana State University Library. Paul is married to the artist Marsha Karle, with whom he has collaborated as author and artist on seven books.